A World of Difference

Hats Off to Hats!

By Sara Corbett

CHILDRENS PRESS®
CHICAGO

Picture Acknowledgments

Cover (top left), NASA; cover (bottom left), © Michael Scott/Tony Stone Images; Cover (top right), © Robert Frerck/Odyssey/Chicago; Cover (bottom right) and 1, © Lee Boltin; 3 (bottom left), © Scott Liles/Unicorn Stock Photos; 3 (top right), © Lee Boltin; 3 (bottom right), © Robert Frerck/Odyssey/Chicago; 4 (left), © Porterfield/Chickering; 4 (top right), © Tom McCarthy/PhotoEdit, 4 (bottom right), © John Elk III; 5 (top left), © Lee Boltin; 5 (top right), © Jean Sloman/Valan; 5 (bottom right), © Wolfgang Kaehler; 6 (bottom), © Sally Mayman/Tony Stone Images; 6 (top), © Cameramann International, Ltd.; 7 (left), © Bachman/PhotoEdit; 7 (top right), © Chip and Rosa Maria de la Cueva Peterson; 7 (bottom right), © Paul Harris/Tony Stone Images; 8 (left), © Susan Malis/MGA/Photri; 8 (right), © Clara Parsons/Valan; 9 (left), © Karen Sherlock/Tony Stone Images; 9 (top right), © Jeff Greenberg/PhotoEdit; 9 (bottom right), Christopher Arnesen/Tony Stone Images; 10 (left), © Jeff Greenberg/Unicorn Stock Photos; 10 (right), © H. Armstrong Roberts; 11 (left), © C. Osborne/Valan; 11 (top right), © Maritius/Photri; 11 (bottom right), © Cameramann International, Ltd.; 12 (left), © Porterfield/Chickering; 12 (bottom right), © Kennon Cooke/Valan; 13 (top left), © Tony Morrison/South American Pictures; 13 (top right), © Chip and Rosa Maria de la Cueva Peterson; 13 (bottom), © Wolfgang Kaehler; 14 (left and right), © Photri; 15 (bottom left), Robert Frerck/ Odyssey/Chicago; 15 (top right), © Tom McCarthy/MGA/Photri; 15 (bottom right), © Wolfgang Kaehler; 16 (left and bottom right), © Robert Frerck/Odyssey/Chicago; 17 (top left), © Virginia R. Grimes; 17 (bottom right), © Lee Boltin; 17 (right), UPI/Bettmann; 18 (left and right), The Bettmann Archive; 19 (top left), © Wolfgang Kaehler; 19 (bottom left), The Bettmann Archive; 19 (right), © Lee Boltin; 20 (left and right), © Photri; 21 (top), © Carl Purcell; 21 (bottom), © Robert Frerck/Odyssey/Chicago; 22 (bottom), © Carl Purcell; 22 (top left), © Wolfgang Kaehler; 22 (top right), © Robert W. Ginn/Photri; 23 (top left), © A. Ramey/Unicorn Stock Photos; 23 (bottom left), © Robert Frerck/Odyssey/Chicago; 23 (right), © Paul Chesley/Tony Stone Images; 24 (left), © Alan Oddie/PhotoEdit; 24 (top right), © Christine Osborne/Valan; 24 (bottom right), © Cameramann International, Ltd.; 25 (top left), © Wolfgang Kaehler; 25 (top right), © David J. Sams/Tony Stone Images; 25 (bottom), © Ken Fisher/Tony Stone Images; 26 (top), © Steve Vidler/SuperStock International, Inc.; 26 (bottom), © Robert Frerck/Odyssey/Chicago; 27 (top left), © Rohan/Tony Stone Images; 27 (bottom left), © Mary Kate Denny/PhotoEdit; 27 (right), © Deborah L. Martin/Unicorn Stock Photos; 28 (left), © Myrleen Ferguson/PhotoEdit; 28 (right), © Dough Armand/Tony Stone Images; 29 (top left), © Christopher Arnesen/Tony Stone Images; 29 (bottom left), © Aneal Vohra/Unicorn Stock Photos; 29 (right), © K. Scholz/H. Armstrong Roberts; 30 (left), © Paul Grebliunas/Tony Stone Images; 30 (right), © Victor Englebert; 31 (top left and top right), © Wolfgang Kaehler; 31 (bottom), UPI/Bettmann

On the cover
Top: Turkish helmet, c. 1500–1800
Bottom left: Quechua girl in traditional dress
Bottom right: Peruvian wool cap, c. 50 B.C.

On the title page
Ashanti chief's hat, Ghana

Project Editor Shari Joffe
Design Herman Adler Design Group
Photo Research Feldman & Associates

Corbett, Sara.
   Hats off to hats / by Sara Corbett.
      p. cm. — (A world of difference)
   Summary: Explores the world of hats, discussing the origin
and function of different kinds found around the world.
   ISBN 0-516-08176-4
   1. Hats — Juvenile literature. [1. Hats.] I. Title.
II. Series.
GT2110.C67 1995
391'.43 — dc20
                                                    95-2394
                                                     CIP
                                                     AC

Contents

A Hat for Every Head

Why do people wear hats? This may seem like a simple question, but there really isn't an easy answer for it. Stop and think a minute about the kind of hats you wear. Do you have a hat to keep you warm in the winter? How about a hat to shade your face from the sun when it's hot out? One reason we wear hats is to protect our heads, faces, and ears from the weather.

But you can also learn a lot about people by looking at the hats they wear. A hat may help you to guess what part of the world somebody comes from, or it can give clues to what a person does for a living. Other hats tell you about someone's beliefs and values. So why do you wear hats? Maybe you wear a baseball cap to show support for your favorite team. Some people like hats because they're a good way to cover up messy hair!

Football helmet, United States Some hats, like sports helmets, are worn to protect the head from physical injury.

Ami tribal woman wearing traditional hat, Taiwan Sometimes a hat signals that a person comes from a certain country or region.

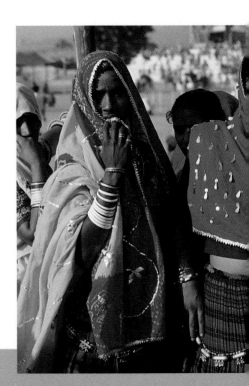

Peruvian wool cap, c. 50 B.C.
This knit cap was made to keep its wearer warm in the chilly Andes mountains of South America.

Masai warrior wearing ostrich-feather hat, Kenya Some hats are worn only during special ceremonies or celebrations.

If you play a sport, you might need a helmet to protect your head from injury. If you belong to a scouting group, you probably have a hat as part of your uniform. Maybe you have a crazy-looking hat that's simply fun to wear! The best thing about hats is that they're often as unique as the individual people who wear them.

Your hat tells the world something about you, whether it's about your interests, your work, your culture, or your mood. What might these hats tell you about the people who wear them?

Railroad conductor, China A hat can tell you what someone's job is. This hat is designed to make the conductor seem a few inches taller, so she will be visible on a crowded train platform.

Women wearing *saris*, India
A hat or head covering may indicate a person's religious beliefs. A Hindu woman typically wears a *sari,* a long robe that doubles as a head covering.

What Makes a Hat?

So where do all these hats come from? Now that we've got big factories and complicated trade routes, our hats are often made by machines, using materials that can come from just about anywhere in the world. In many places today, you can walk down the street and buy a hat made of Chinese silk or Norwegian wool. But before we had factories and stores, people had to make their hats from materials readily available in their surroundings. And to this day, many people still make hats using the resources they have on hand. For one thing, homemade hats are a nice way of upholding tradition. Also, the materials native to an environment often make the best hats!

For instance, the Carib people of Guyana have discovered that the stretchy outer shell of the palm blossom makes a perfect lightweight hat. They cut the shell off one of the many available palm trees and can pull it right over their heads. Presto! It's an instant, nifty hat!

Shell cap, Papua New Guinea
This woman lives in the Chambri Lakes region of Papua New Guinea, where seashells are plentiful.

Leaf hat, Zaire

Indonesian dancer wearing flower hat On the island of Bali, dancers wear hats made of leather and covered with fresh tropical flowers. Before every performance, dancers need to pick themselves a new hat!

Palm leaf hats, Puerto Rico These hats are made from palm leaves, which are plentiful in Puerto Rico.

Reindeer herder, Siberia Reindeer herders in the Siberian Arctic use the fur of their animals to make warm, protective hats and other clothing.

Staying Warm, Staying Cool

The kind of hat we wear usually has a lot to do with the type of climate we live in. If you look at hats from different parts of the world, you will see that almost every one corresponds to the natural conditions of its home country. A hat that is considered useful and good-looking in one country might seem totally silly in another country.

Wool cap, Portugal Like the *chullo*, this cap has protective ear flaps to keep out the cold and wind.

For instance, imagine that you lived in a small village in the South American country of Ecuador. Do you think you'd wear blue jeans, eat pancakes, or play video games? Probably not! More likely, you'd wear a wool poncho, eat a grain called quinoa, and herd sheep in the Andes mountains. Instead of wearing a baseball cap or ski hat, you'd have a large-brimmed hat made of stiffened llama's wool to protect you from the harsh wind and snow of the mountains.

Chullo, **Peru** A stocking cap made from llama wool, the *chullo* is specially shaped to keep a person's ears nice and toasty in the chilly Andes mountains of South America.

Yupik woman wearing squirrel parka, Alaska People who live in the Arctic, where it is extremely cold much of the year, often rely on hats and coats made from the fur of such nearby animals as caribou, seal, walrus, and squirrel.

Russian *shapka* Made from sheepskin, this hat helps people stay warm during long Russian winters.

Sami woman, Lapland The Sami people live in far-northern Europe above the arctic circle. Sami women wear tight-fitting wool bonnets that cover their ears.

Now imagine wearing an enormous llama-wool hat the next time you go to school. What would happen? People would probably think it was strange, wouldn't they? Well, if you wore a baseball cap while herding sheep in the Andes, you'd get strange looks, too. And your ears would freeze! This is an example of how hats "fit" the part of the world they come from.

By looking at people's hats, we can guess at what kind of environment they live in. You won't find a heavy, fur cap in a sunny place like Jamaica, nor would a straw hat last very long in a windy, wintry place such as Siberia.

Tuareg man, Algeria The Tuareg are a nomadic people who live in the Sahara—a huge desert in northern Africa. They wrap their turbans around their head and face so that only their eyes are exposed to the harsh sun and sandstorms of the desert.

Arab man wearing *Ghurtra*, Israel The *ghurtra* is made from lightweight cotton. It not only shades a person's head from the intense sun of the desert, it offers protection from the sandstorms that frequently whip up.

Fishermen, Denmark
These traditional fishing caps can take a beating during rough ocean storms.

***Tarboosh,* Kenya** This cotton cap is white for a reason: the color will reflect the sun's light rather than absorb it. White clothing is therefore very popular in countries near the equator.

Straw hat, China Wide-brimmed straw hats are very popular in Asian countries, where the sun can be extremely tiring.

Hat Connections

Sometimes your hat can tell the world about your connections to other people. For instance, if you play on an athletic team, you and your teammates might wear the same color and type of hat. In this way, hats can help signal to the world that a group of people is proudly united. Hats can also serve as a badge, identifying your connections in terms of marriage, family, hometown, or whose side of a dispute you're on.

Certain decorative hats are worn in some countries as a tradition. In Scotland, for example, men wear the tam-o'-shanter, a heavy wool cap with a large pom-pom on top. The caps are made from fabrics in different colorful plaid patterns. Each extended family, or "clan," has its own unique pattern; so you can identify what "clan" someone belongs to just by looking at his tam-o'-shanter!

Marine cadets, Canada Military groups wear matching hats to help them feel united, since pride can help overcome fear—and fear can be a soldier's worst enemy. Also, during a battle, everyone needs to know who is on which side!

Tam-o'-shanter, Scotland The tam-o'-shanter helped people to express their unity as members of an extended family, or clan.

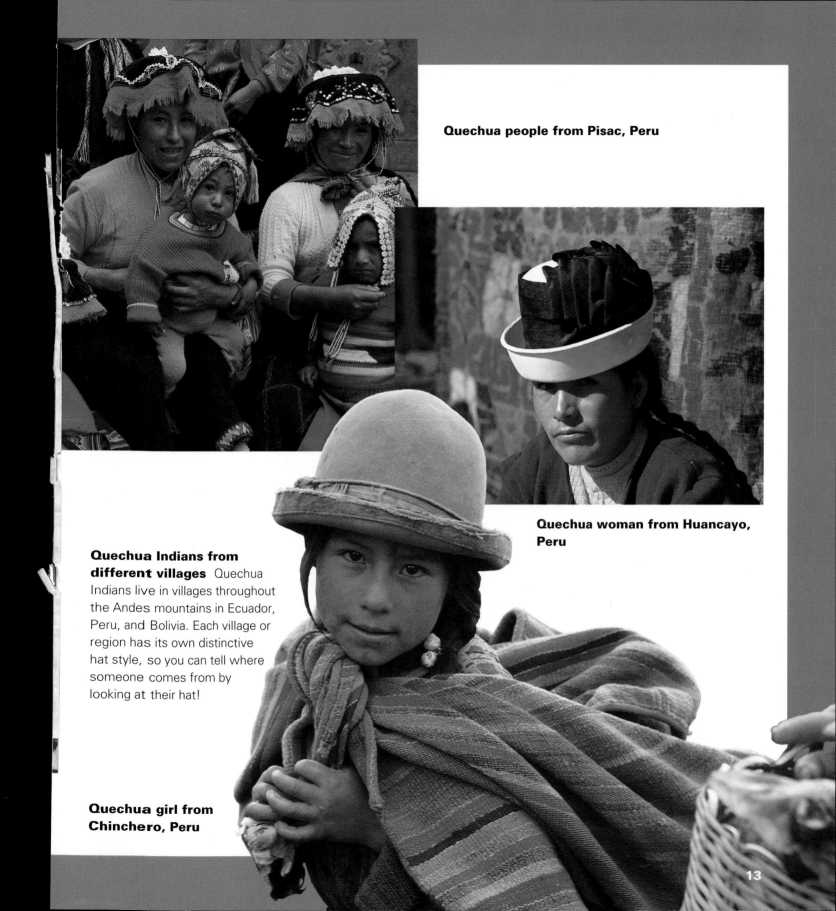

Quechua people from Pisac, Peru

Quechua woman from Huancayo, Peru

Quechua Indians from different villages Quechua Indians live in villages throughout the Andes mountains in Ecuador, Peru, and Bolivia. Each village or region has its own distinctive hat style, so you can tell where someone comes from by looking at their hat!

Quechua girl from Chinchero, Peru

13

Yao women and children, Thailand The Yao are a mountain-dwelling people who live in southern China and Southeast Asia.

In many parts of the world, people wear a certain kind of hat to show that they belong to a particular ethnic group or clan. Such hats may have been worn by the group for hundreds or even thousands of years. These two pages show several examples of traditional ethnic hats.

Zulu woman and child, South Africa

Hakka woman, Hong Kong
The Hakka are a group of North Chinese who migrated to South China in the 1270s. Their name means "guest people." Even today, they have maintained their traditional customs and speak a different form of Chinese than others in southern China.

Weaver from Nebaj, Guatemala Many Indians in Guatemala wear beautiful hand-woven fabrics. Each village has its own designs and colors. By looking at the pattern a man is wearing, you can tell what village he's from, what family he is in, if he's married, how many children he has, and if his children are married!

Batak man, Indonesia

How High is Your Hat?

Throughout history, people around the globe have used hats to show their power or status in society. What is the most important part of a king or queen's outfit? The crown! Leaders have worn crowns for thousands of years, beginning with the earliest kings of Egypt, who wore tall crowns made of stiff reed frames wrapped in cloth. In China and other parts of Asia, men have traditionally worn hats with golf-ball-sized knobs on top. The knobs can be made from anything from ruby to wood, and the value of the knob is supposed to signify its owner's position within the community.

Ancient Egyptian crown

Golden helmet, Turkey, 1500–1800 Throughout history, people have displayed their wealth or power by wearing hats that are elaborately decorated or include expensive materials. This helmet, made of gold and inlaid with precious gems, would have been worn by a high-ranking member of Turkish society.

Lion's mane headdress, Tanzania When a young Masai warrior in Tanzania kills his first lion, he becomes a more important member of his tribe and receives a ceremonial headdress made from the lion's mane.

Queen Elizabeth II of England

Ashanti chief's hat, Ghana
This hat is made of antelope leather and is covered with gold ornaments.

In Europe and the United States, the top hat was the most popular men's hat to be found during the 18th and 19th centuries. These tall hats were supposed to symbolize the dignity and importance of the people who wore them. Women, too, during that time reflected their wealth and power through large, elaborately plumed hats. The bigger and taller your hat was, the more important you were supposed to be. Interestingly enough, most of these "power" hats were famous for being uncomfortable to wear!

To this day, certain political figures choose their hats carefully, making sure the hat will command the respect a person needs to be an effective leader.

Top hat The top hat, also known as the "stove pipe," "chimney pot," or "topper," became popular during the 1800s. It was the favorite hat of the rich and powerful in Europe and the United States for many years.

15th-century French hennin Only women of the upper classes in European society wore hennins—towering, cone-shaped headdresses. The reason for this was that hennins were so tall and heavy, a woman needed several servants to even walk with one on!

Indian turban In India, the color of a turban, as well as the way it is wound, indicates a person's social status.

Still other people have chosen hats that display their resistance to certain political ideas or situations. The beret has been the hat of choice for a number of famous rebels, including an important Cuban revolutionary named Che Guevara.

Powerful plumage Feathers of all shapes, sizes, and colors could be found in the extravagant hats of wealthy women. In the late 1880s, at least five million American birds were being killed each year to supply the hat business. Plumed hats lost their appeal in the early 1900s, when people campaigned against them to protect birds.

Dakota headdress The Dakota people traditionally lived on the North American plains. A Dakota man's position in society was determined by his skill in warfare. The bravest warriors earned the right to wear bonnets of eagle feathers.

19

Hats and Beliefs

For some people, the fact that hats sit on top of our heads makes them more special than any other item of clothing. What could be the reason for this? A hat reaches toward the sky, which is considered in many cultures to be the realm of spirits. So it becomes important for certain hats to present a good "face" to the heavens.

In Peru, the descendants of the ancient Incas consider themselves to be "children of the sun." Their way of paying respect to the sun god is to wear a large bowl-shaped hat called a *montera* that symbolizes and points toward the sun. The Annamese people of central Vietnam wear an open form of the turban, leaving the tops of their heads exposed to the sky, so that good spirits will know they have an open invitation to drop in and out of the turban-wearers' bodies any time!

Tribal woman wearing traditional headdress, Thailand This cone-shaped headdress is meant to reflect the architectural shape of a Buddhist shrine.

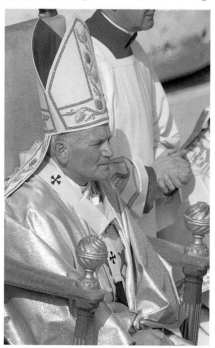

Papal hat The height of the Roman Catholic Pope's hat symbolizes his soul soaring toward heaven.

Tasseled Greek cap Traditionally, a tassel on a cap was thought to guard against demons. Around the world, tassels have represented protection from evil. This is how they became popular attachments not only to hats, but to pillows, curtains, and swords, too.

Montera, **Peru** The *montera* is worn by some men and women in the Andes mountains of Peru. Their ancestors, the Inca, are believed to have descended from the sun.

Other hats are meant to represent spiritual values, like faithfulness and humility. The fez is a plain felt cap that not only reaches upward, but is also undecorated and simple to show that its wearer is devoted to the Muslim god, Allah. In the United States during the 1800s, women of the Quaker faith wore simple "sugar scoop" bonnets that covered their hair completely to demonstrate modesty, which was a central part of their religion.

***Chadri,* Morocco** Women throughout the Near- and Middle East have traditionally worn veils like this *chadri* to cover their heads and faces completely. The roots of this tradition come from the Muslim faith, which dictates that a veil will protect a woman from the "evil eye," commonly known as the male gaze.

Amish bonnet The Amish, members of a devout Protestant sect, live in communities in the northeastern and midwestern United States. The simple bonnets worn by Amish women reflect the importance of modesty in the beliefs of the Amish.

Some hats work as a sort of "spiritual helmet," designed to ward off the influences of evil. In Haiti, for example, some people wear straw "voodoo hats," which are meant to protect them from spells cast by voodoo priests. Because it is thought that evil spirits cannot cross water, there is a squiggly line running around the brim of the Haitian protective hat. The line represents a river to keep the evil spirits away from the hat-wearer's head!

Muslim fez Muslim men wear brimless fezes or skullcaps because the Islamic faith dictates that nothing should get in the way of someone's view of heaven.

Jewish males wearing *yarmulkes*, Israel During worship, Jewish males are supposed to cover their heads with a *yarmulke,* also called a *kipa.* Some religious Jewish men wear a *yarmulke* all day, because they believe themselves to be in the presence of God at all times.

Women attending Christian church service, Tahiti Wearing a hat in church is a sign of respect.

Guatemalan headpiece The Santiago women of Guatemala wear a band wrapped around their heads thirteen times. Not only is thirteen a magical number in their tradition, but the band also has portraits of the ancient Mayan wind and cloud gods woven into it.

Hats and Work

Nurse, Zimbabwe This cap is clean and crisp, imitating the ideal environment for healing.

Hats are often linked to the jobs we perform. A firefighter wears one hat, while a chef wears another. Can you imagine cooking gourmet meals in a heavy-duty fire hat? Or fighting a blazing fire in a crisp white chef's hat? It probably wouldn't work very well, since our work hats are specifically suited to our roles.

If someone changes hats, she or he is probably changing roles. This is why we say someone who does a lot of different things is a person who "wears many hats." Have you ever had someone tell you to "hang up the hat"? What they're saying is that you should call it quits, at least for a while. At the end of a long, hard day, most people are quite ready to hang up their work hats!

Palace guard, Nepal A special hat and uniform helps gives a guard a look of authority.

"Bobby," England Throughout the world, police officers wear special hats or helmets so that they can be easily recognized.

Flower sellers, Senegal These women will allow you to buy flowers right off their hats!

Firefighter, United States
This helmet is designed to protect a firefighter's head and neck from heat and flame.

Venetian gondolier In the city of Venice, Italy, men who steer the long gondolas down narrow canals wear these straw hats during the warm summer months. A red ribbon means the gondolier has at least five years' experience.

Zulu rickshaw driver, South Africa In South Africa, Zulu rickshaw drivers can be recognized by their colorful headdresses, which are made from ox horns and bird feathers. These headdresses are supposed to give the driver, who spends long days towing heavy passenger loads, the traveling powers of bird and beast.

Gaucho, **Argentina** *Gauchos* were the legendary cowboys of the *pampas,* or grasslands, of Argentina and Uruguay. They flourished from the mid-1700s to the mid-1800s. Since traditional *gauchos* lived outdoors, they needed a hat like this, which would hold up in everything from dust to driving rain.

Moroccan water sellers

In Morocco, most rural people do their shopping at the local *souk,* or market. Water sellers, who are easy to spot because of their distinctive traditional outfits, can be found in most Moroccan markets.

Chef, Japan The traditional chef's hat has exactly 100 pleats in it, signifying the number of different ways a topnotch chef can prepare an egg.

Factory worker, United States
Hard hats are essential for people who do work that could be dangerous.

Put on Your Party Hat!

Hip hip hooray! Hip hip hooray! Hip hip HOO-RAY!

What do we do after we finish cheering? We throw our hats into the air! This helps us to express our joy or excitement about a special event. Hats are an important part of parties, festivals, and ceremonies all over the world.

Many people like to wear festive hats to mark special occasions. In most cultures, a wedding is a very important celebration, and it's common for both brides and grooms to wear special hats on their wedding day.

Up, up, and away!
It's become a tradition in the United States for high-school and college graduates to throw their hats in the air to celebrate the end of the graduation ceremony.

All decked out for Carnival, Trindidad
Carnival, celebrated in many countries, is a week of festivity before Lent, the Christian period of repentance that begins on Ash Wednesday and ends on Easter. Dressing up in wild costumes has long been part of the tradition of Carnival.

Ceremonial headdresses, Papua New Guinea Magnificent headdresses are an important part of many ceremonies and festivals in Papua New Guinea.

Tsumo-kakushi, **Japan**
This bridal hat is meant to symbolize the beauty, purity, and majesty of the bride. It is so large and heavy that often a woman cannot even walk a few steps in it without somebody to help her along.

"Light Queen" St. Lucia's Day is a Swedish folk celebration held on December 13, one of the shortest days of the year. It features a ceremony with a "Light Queen," who, in her white gown and crown of lighted candles, represents the returning sun.

Hats Express

One of the most exciting things about hats is that there are really no limits to what they can be. Sometimes, hats don't have any meaning at all—they're worn just for decoration, to make a person feel stylish and attractive!

And there are so many different kinds of hats to wear! In the fashion world, hats are being created constantly to express new trends and artistic concepts. As technology, jobs, and cultures change, new hats are designed to match the changes. These days you will find American hats being worn in Africa, and African hats being worn in Japan. As our systems of communication and transportation grow, we are able to share ideas across cultures and great distances.

Bai woman, China

Guambiano Indian boys, Colombia

Massalla women and children, Mali

Vietnamese cowboys

American high-fashion hat, 1950s

While hats can represent your heritage or nationality, they can also celebrate the unique and individual spirit that makes you who you are!

Glossary

ancient very old (p.20)

correspond to be in agreement with (p.8)

culture the beliefs and customs of a group of people that are passed from one generation to another (p.5)

custom the usual way of doing things (p.15)

descendants the children of an ancestor (p.20)

devoted completely loyal (p.22)

distinctive clearly marking a person or thing as different from others (p.13)

effective able to produce the proper result (p.18)

elaborate having much detail (p.16)

equator an imaginary circle around the earth that is equally distant from the north pole and south pole (p.11)

essential necessary (p.27)

ethnic group a group of people whose members share the same culture, language, or customs (p.14)

faithfulness the quality of being loyal or true to another person (p.22)

gondola a long narrow boat used in the canals of Venice, Italy (p.25)

gourmet an expert in food and drink (p.24)

heritage something that is passed on from one's ancestors (p.31)

humility the quality of not being proud (p.22)

native born, grown, or originating in a particular place or country (p.6)

nomadic referring to people who move from place to place (p.10)

plumed having feathers (p.18)

recognized identified (p.24)

repentance a feeling of regret for having done somethng wrong (p.28)

resource a supply of something that can be used or drawn on (p.6)

rickshaw a two or three-wheeled vehicle pulled by a human (p.26)

status position or rank (p.16)

symbolize to stand for or represent something (p.18)

technology the scientific methods and ideas used in industry and trade (p.30)

traditional handed down from generation to generation (p.4)

unique one of a kind (p.5)

values the beliefs, standards, or principles held by a person or group of people (p.22)

Index

About the Author

Sara Corbett is a writer who lives in Santa Fe, New Mexico. This book is for her friend Mike, who wears a lucky baseball cap almost everywhere he goes.